HOW THE BRAIN FEELS
Working with Emotion and Cognition

Wayfinder Press
London, England

Copyright © 2012 Philip Harland

ISBN 978-0-9561607-3-7

The right of Philip Harland to be identified as the author and illustrator of this work has been asserted in accordance with the UK Copyright, Designs, and Patents Act 1988

All rights reserved

With the exception of brief quotations, no part of this publication may be reproduced or transmitted in any form or by any means without the permission in writing of the copyright holder and publisher

All enquiries to info@wayfinderpress.co.uk

Let my heart be wise. It is the gods' best gift.
Euripides

Contents

INTRODUCTION page	7
Emotion and Evolution	7
Emotion and Intelligence	8
Emotion and Cognition	9
Emotion and Definition	9
Emotional Management	10
The Structure of Emotion	11
End Notes	12
PART I AROUSAL	13
Impetus	14
Importance	14
The Associative Tendency	15
Exercise in Emotional Arousal	16
Feelings Are Ever Present	17
Conclusion	18
End Notes	18
PART II SENSATION	19
Confusion of Feeling	20
What Are Emotions/Feelings?	21
Exercise in Sensation #1	22
Anger	22
Excitement, Joy, Fear	23
Sensation and Emotion	24
Exercise in Sensation #2	26
Sensation and Construction	27
Sensation and Metaphor	27
Emotion as Metaphor	28
Facilitating Metaphor	29
Exercise in Sensation #3	30
End Notes	30
PART III CONSTRUCTION	31
Emotions Don't Just Happen	31
Emotional Conditioning	32
Novel and Conditioned Feelings	33
The Construction of Emotion	33
Direct and Indirect Feelings	34
Sensory Acuity	36
Felt and Interpreted Feelings	38
Changing Feelings	39
Case History: Janet	40
End Notes	41
PART IV APPRAISAL	42
Feelings Tell Us How We Are Doing	43
Phases of Appraisal	44
Hamlet & the Recursivity Syndrome	45
Reason Is Nowhere Pure	46
Appraising Values	46
Fear Has The Largest Eyes of All	47
The Neurophysiology of Fear	48
Case History: Clare	49
End Notes	51
PART V VOLITION	52
Acting on Impulse	53
Involuntary Impulse	54
Working with Somatic Markers	54
Working with Micro Emotions	56
Working with Metaphor	57
Metaphor in Emotional Management	58
Voluntary Impulse	59
Deconditioning Therapies	59
Reprogramming Therapies	60
Transforming Therapies	61
Case History: Ben	61
Concluding	64
End Notes	65
Acknowledgments	66
References and Further Reading	66
Author	66

INTRODUCTION

> Models of facilitation (therapy, counselling, teaching, coaching, health management, etc.) have rarely dealt with the inter-dependency of emotion and cognition. In the 1980s, NLP researchers developed the concept of the structure of emotion (make a conscious change to a sub-modality of a feeling and you can change the feeling itself). Work in the 1990s on 'Meta-States' addressed the modulating of primary emotional states with cognitively led meta-levels of feeling. Here we explore the neurolinguistic basis of *emotional intelligence,* relating recent research on the structure and relationship of emotion and cognition to David Grove's work in Clean Language and Therapeutic Metaphor.

A Greek poet writes of a woman who has waited more than twenty years for her beloved husband to return home. He embraces her passionately. She is cautious and anxious, unsure of him. He is upset. She is sorrowful. He is angry. She is fearful. So Homer in The Odyssey describes the reunion of Penelope and Odysseus in terms we can readily understand today. In three thousand years the language of the emotions has hardly changed. It may not have changed much in six million years.

EMOTION AND EVOLUTION

After all these years of human evolution, how far have we come in terms of our emotional development?

The costs of emotional dysfunction – the inability to respond appropriately to our emotions – can be counted many times over in the worst effects of anger, addiction, fear, anxiety, depression, intolerance, fanaticism, and sociogenic illness.[1] Emotional dysfunction is contagious. Indeed, the word 'pathology', study of disease, comes from the Greek word *pathologia*, study of the emotions. Disease of the emotions can be passed from generation to generation. Doctors calculate that one in five of the children they see has emotional stress-related problems.

A particular kind of dysfunction – lack of sympathy for the feelings of others – is readily programmed into vulnerable people by psychopaths who bluff or bully their way into positions of corporate, religious, or political power.

It's not all doom and gloom, however. As relative newcomers (there were four thousand million years of life on earth before we appeared a mere six million years ago), perhaps we are not doing badly. Compassion, joy, altruism, and sympathy are in plentiful evidence. And we know that every negative emotion, however vexatious, has a positive intention, or may be useful in some situations, or may be a signpost to a meaningful value.

Where do we want to be emotionally? The development of emotional sensibility is a necessary prerequisite for reducing fear and violence in society; for helping us live and work well with our fellows; for managing change; for using intuition creatively; and for developing the learning potential of the human mind.

So what has to happen? What further adaptation do we need to make in order to thrive? It has always been easy for us to think we think. But now how do we think we feel?

EMOTION AND INTELLIGENCE
After all these years of heartache and joy, we could be ready to take a huge evolutionary step in emotional intelligence as we begin to recognize what is generally accepted nowadays among neuro-scientists – that emotions are not independent of the brain; they are functions of the brain.[2] They are constructed and represented in that tangled web, and have a direct inter-relationship with its cognitive functions. The mind produces feeling as much as thought. To grasp this fact and to accept its implications is to make a giant stride on the road to taking responsibility for ourselves.

It may no longer be useful to separate emotion and cognition in the conventional way, because far from interfering with rationality, as we have traditionally maintained, a sense of emotionality is increasingly cherished as necessary for reason to operate usefully.

EMOTION AND COGNITION

To talk of emotion is to talk of a brain function arising directly from information input and to talk of cognition is to talk of a brain function arising *in*directly from input. We shall discuss this in more detail later, but if you would like a simple distinction for now, that is it. Disengaging thinking from feeling is like trying to separate light and shade, or the crest and trough of a wave. The difference between them could hardly be more obvious, yet one cannot exist without the other. I invite you, therefore, to make the direct / indirect distinction:

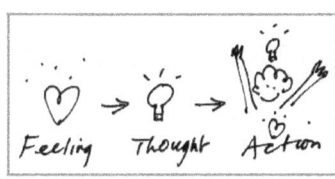

Feeling (direct) comes first. Thinking (indirect) comes after. The urge to mental or physical activity that results derives from a combination of the two.

You might like to believe that there is such a thing as 'pure' reason, or 'abstract' thinking – the kind mathematicians or philosophers are said to employ. Well, rational thinkers are not cyphers. There has to be an emotional motivation behind – or rather, before – any intellectual activity. A desire to know more, the frustration of not knowing, excitement at the challenge, envy of a rival mathematician or philosopher, and so on.

EMOTION AND DEFINITION

Just as we can make distinctions between emotion and cognition, we can also make them between 'emotion' and 'feeling', and 'feeling' and 'sensation'. The differences are largely academic and researchers vary in their attempts to characterize them. In fact, a great deal of ambiguity surrounds all our words about feelings, which is hardly surprising given our invariably subjective and frequently equivocal experience of what the words represent.

This ambiguity of meaning may relate to the notion that one cannot have *any* experiential sense, including an emotion, without *at the same time* (it happens so quickly, it seems to be at the same time) interpreting it. And interpretation, wilful or not, is a cognitive act. Ergo: the thought about the feeling *is* the feeling. This is one of those academic distinctions! Meanwhile for the sake of a shared understanding, here are my working definitions, gathered from an assortment of sources.

COGNITION	A broad term applied to those mental activities related to thinking, conceiving, or reasoning, where the underlying characteristics involve symbolizing, imagery, memory, belief, intentionality, insight, judgment, problem-solving, etc.
EMOTION	Subjectively experienced moving, stirring or agitated mental state or feeling. Sometimes limited to the strongly felt 'basic' emotions ('sad', 'glad', 'mad', 'bad'), and often used interchangeably with:
FEELING	A consciousness of, or belief about, something in the bodymind. Can be distinguished from, but is also used interchangeably with:
SENSATION	An experience, or awareness, of conditions within or outside the body produced by the stimulation of a sensory receptor or receptor system.
MOOD	A relatively short-term state of the feelings.
STATE	A combination of any or all of the above at a given moment.

EMOTIONAL MANAGEMENT

One of the expectations on me as a Clean Language facilitator is to be able to acknowledge and facilitate the thoughts, beliefs, judgments, emotions, sensations, and moods (the 'states') of my clients without complicating them with my own. In order to have the remotest chance of doing this, I have had to become familiar with my own beliefs and feelings. I have had to recognize, name, and manage them. And I have especially needed to understand them in relation to my cognitions, with which I have generally been more familiar. This paper is a further stage of that journey. In my childhood, the theatre of the emotions was a desolate place. Feelings hovered in ghostly silence in the wings or erupted in inexplicable explosions backstage. The whole thing was a mystery. As Matthew Arnold wrote:

> *And we are here as a darkling plain*
> *Swept with confused alarms of struggle and flight,*
> *Where ignorant armies clash by night.*

One of the reasons people go into therapy – as clients or therapists – is because they feel, or think, that their feeling and thinking are somehow opposed. Passion and intelligence are ignorant armies in a permanent state of attrition. Acknowledging the conflict is a necessary preamble to the negotiations the parties must enter before peace can prevail. It may also help to know that emotions don't just happen; they are constructed over time. This is normally a very short period of time, a fraction of a second, but it can be broken down into five distinct parts that make the problems associated with difficult feelings more amenable to intervention.

THE STRUCTURE OF EMOTION

Stage 1
AROUSAL
Instigating stimuli
How the emotional process gets going.
What sets it off.

Stage 2
SENSATION
Physiological correlates
What emotions actually are.
How we know we have them.

Stage 3
CONSTRUCTION
Systemic coherence
How emotions are created in the bodymind.
How they inter-relate with cognitions.

Stage 4
APPRAISAL
Cognitive evaluation
How we consider and communicate our emotions and cognitions. How we may track them in others.

Stage 5
VOLITION
Motivational impulse
The urge to act. What happens as a result of arousal, sensation, construction, and appraisal.

A sixth stage, ACTION (physical or mental), will be the outcome of this five-part process. Here is a personal example. It happened over a period of days, but the stages are much the same as in feeling-thoughts that happen in an instant. Recently I realized I was seeing a number of clients who were angry and others who were phobic (1 AROUSAL). It stimulated a complex of physiological activity in my body and brain (2 SENSATION). I characterized this as a gap in my knowledge of anger, fear, and emotions in general, and felt frustrated, anxious, and incompetent as a result (3 CONSTRUCTION). Thinking about this, I became curious and excited at the prospect of learning more as I realized I could neutralize the feelings that I didn't like and enhance those I did (4 APPRAISAL). I was moved to do something in order to improve my knowledge and understanding (5 VOLITION). I went off researching and wrote up my findings (6 ACTION). Doing this helped me feel useful and fulfilled.

Whether the behaviours that follow from our experience of a feeling-thought are beneficial or not will largely depend on the degree of emotional intelligence involved. Emotional intelligence is simply learning to use our emotions intelligently and this happens when the brain's amygdala and cortex are able to communicate well as one circuit. (There is more about the neurophysiology in Parts III and IV.)

The existence of a five-part structure to feeling allows the possibility of intervening at some point before the feeling becomes disabling. The question then becomes, at what point and how? How can a fraction of a second be extended to allow clients access to the information they need in order to feel better rather than worse?

The rest of this paper goes further into the stages of Arousal, Sensation, Construction, Appraisal, and Volition, and offers an answer to the question.

Notes to the Introduction

1 *Sociogenic illness*: genuine symptoms induced by fear and anxiety. Three weeks after the World Trade Center attacks, 35 people suffered nausea, headache and sore throat after a man sprayed what turned out to be window cleaner into a Maryland subway station.

2 *Emotions as functions of the brain* in its association with the body. More on the emotional bodymind in Parts II and III.

| AROUSAL | SENSATION | CONSTRUCTION | APPRAISAL | VOLITION |
| Part I | Part II | Part III | Part IV | Part V |

Part I AROUSAL

We have hearts within.
Warm, live, improvident, indecent hearts.
Elizabeth Barrett Browning

What arouses feeling? It used to be thought that emotions, like surplus food, were the privilege of the rich and that essentially they came from nowhere. Modern theories recognize that they are neither a luxury nor a metaphysical event. As soon as we have *any* experience, we become emotionally aroused to a greater or lesser extent. The instigating stimuli will either be exogenous (events out there in the world), or endogenous (internal thoughts and sensations). An example of exogenous stimuli: when I saw pictures of the terrorist attacks on New York, I felt shocked and anxious. Endogenous: when I imagined the suffering of the victims, I felt wretched and angry.[1]

As living beings, we are in a repeatedly reconstructed state of constant flux. We have no choice but to take in a near-infinite number of bits of information from the world in every moment of our waking lives. These stimuli have an emotional and physiological effect beyond our immediate control.

When you came to this page you were in that most basic form of consciousness, a feeling state of some kind, whether you were conscious of it or not. As you read now, your brain is changing. It is making many millions of unconscious neural connections, associating your present seeing and hearing to what you have already seen and heard in your life. And you will now be in a different emotional state to the one you were in a few moments ago. It could be slightly different or entirely different. We are always in a state of feeling *something*.

IMPETUS

Again I ask myself how I come to be exploring emotion and cognition at this time. What were the stimuli that set off the emotional chain of events that resulted in this cognitive activity?

I was working with several clients who seemed to have something in common (*exogenous arousal*) ... these experiences stimulated a process of pattern-spotting in me about emotions (*endogenous arousal*) ... which activated some underlying physiology (*sensation*) ... resulting in a half-conscious awareness of frustration at my own ignorance (*emotional construction*) ... followed by conscious curiosity at the prospect of learning more (*emotional and cognitive appraisal*) ... leading to the impulse to act (*volition*) ... by researching and writing (*action*).[2]

IMPORTANCE

Emotional intelligence is arguably the most important of our multiple intelligences – verbal, spatial, kinesthetic, etc. Being able to track our own and others' emotional life, understanding the multiple causes of feelings, recognizing the distinction between feeling and behaviour, and being able to nurture the emotional growth of others, particularly the young, is of enormous developmental benefit and evolutionary advantage.

If the human condition has been one of underlying fear, frustration, and anxiety for the past six million years or so, as some evolutionary psychologists believe, it really is time we did something about it. Plato said that passions and fears made it impossible for him to think.[3] 2,400 years later, I have no difficulty imagining how he felt. We have inherited more ways of being angry and fearful than we need for survival in the 21st century.

Most of us believe that when we think, we think logically; that is, we use reason in an orderly, unemotional way. One thing I expect to show in this paper is that THE BRAIN CANNOT DISTINGUISH BETWEEN FEELING AND THINKING. This is a logical assertion (i.e., it is perfectly rational), but not everyone will assess it as credible. Indeed, you may have a certainty that it's perfect tosh. "Of course I know the difference," you might well be saying, "between my thoughts and my feelings."

While most of us allow that our feelings are subjective, we claim to be entirely capable of thinking objectively. In fact, if the complexity of bodybrain events we interpret as 'feeling' and 'thinking' occur largely unconsciously, as neuroscience has shown, we can have no idea how, when, or whether we have crossed any hypothetical divide between them, because the direct (feeling) function of the brain and its indirect (thinking) function have no physical threshold. We cannot step from one and be unequivocally in the other. Feeling and thinking are complex neural processes that are to most intents and purposes indistinguishable.

The importance of work on emotion and cognition by Damasio (1994), Goleman (1996), LeDoux (1998), Greenfield (2001) and others is, I believe, this: if none of us is truly capable of distinguishing our emotions from our cognitions, how can we help but fall victim to what LeDoux calls "the Associative Tendency"?

In therapists, coaches, medical professionals and others, this finds its expression in the employment of unconscious personal associations in the interpretation of client meaning, resulting in speculative, subjective, or theory-led interventions. The inevitable result is the contamination of the client's emotional, conceptual, and metaphorical processes by the therapist's own.

Member of the Associative Tendency

What associations did you make to the characters in the drawing? Which did you think was the therapist and which the client? What inferences did you make about their relationship? What kind of people did think they were?

If we can make all this up in an instant about a drawing, think how readily we get up to it with real people. Our brains have no choice but to construct these fantasies, but as Clean facilitators we can make conscious choices about what we do about them.

> We can *allow* our fantasies – without at the same time allowing them to pervert our intentions or shape our behaviour towards the client.
>
> We can *acknowledge* our fantasies – bringing the unacknowledged into consciousness and admitting it as a highly inaccurate metaphor for the client's model of the world.
>
> We can *redirect* our fantasies – so that they relate directly to, and are constantly updated by, the specifics of the client's information and not to our subjective, speculative beliefs and judgments about that information.

How? Knowing more about our own emotions is essential for developing emotional intelligence.

EXERCISE IN EMOTIONAL AROUSAL
Consider your emotional history

- What are the first strong feelings you remember in yourself?

- What are the first strong feelings you were aware of in others?

- Was it encouraged, tolerated, or unacceptable to express feelings openly during your upbringing?

- If encouraged, how did you learn to manage them usefully? If unacceptable, how did you learn to deal with them?

- How would you characterize your prime carers emotionally?

- What would you say were your prime carers' core/basic/ underlying emotional states, the ones they reverted to typically?

- And what are yours?

FEELINGS ARE EVER PRESENT
Seeing's believing, but feeling's the truth.   Thomas Fuller

In Part II, SENSATION, we shall consider *what* feelings are – information signals? bodily responses? powerful manifestations of evolutionary drives? things we all know about until asked to define? Or are they, as neuroscientist Joseph LeDoux claims, just another kind of cognition? What all sensations have in common is that when we describe them, we almost without exception speak in metaphor. *I have a gut feeling. My heart is broken. Happy as a lark. Blind with rage.* Expressions like these are not chosen arbitrarily. What has to be true for a client to encode their description of a sensation in a certain symbolic way rather than another? And what happens if a facilitator believes that the client's metaphors and their own correspond or are comparable?

That seething morass of brain circuitry
configured by personal experiences
and constantly updated
as we live out each moment.   Susan Greenfield

How does the brain feel? Part III, CONSTRUCTION, will track the sequence of events in the bodymind as the dual pathways of emotion and cognition are constructed. A representation of the physical sequence of events will help us assess possible places for intervention. The more aware we are of unconscious processes, the better we will be able to calibrate their effects in consciousness. An analysis of the symbolic construction of feeling will reveal clues about the way emotional problems and their solutions are coded in the unconscious.

I wish thar was winders to my sole, sed I,
so that you could see some of my feelins.   Artemus Ward

Emotions are notoriously difficult to verbalize. In Part IV, APPRAISAL, we consider the process of evaluation, one of the most advanced and misleading functions of the human brain. We will review the choices we make about expressing or suppressing its results and consider how as facilitators we may track these events before intervening. We will particularly evaluate nonverbal appraisal: the (generally) obvious, where the client marks out aspects of their unconscious construction of an emotional landscape by gesture and posture as they speak; and the (generally) less obvious, those tiny twitches of the musculature that signal the appearance of an emotional reaction in the fraction of a second before cognition intervenes. What happens in the micro-moment just after a facilitator's question before the client's brain can appraise it?

*Emotions by their very nature
lead to an impulse to act.*   Joseph LeDoux

Part V, VOLITION, will note that if emotions lead to, or are, the impulse to act, they are the motivators, not prescribers, of action. They do not control what we do. The brain can be trained to reappraise. We will consider how the phenomenon of unconscious volition works, how it relates to the bodymind's innate capacity for healing, and how that may be energized to allow the client more feeling, cognitive, and behavioural choices.

CONCLUSION
*Cognition is not as logical as it was once thought
and emotions are not always so illogical.*   Joseph LeDoux

Many of us will share the view that a cognitive understanding of the neurobiological mechanisms behind emotions is perfectly compatible with a sentimental view of their value to us as human beings. Plato was wrong in this particular: passions do not make it impossible to think. Emotions are as cognitive as any other mental function and they are ours to utilize and enjoy.

With conscious access to the way our brains construct feeling and thought, we can make better use of their interdependence. We are one system. Just as we can choose (if not always easily) what to think, we can choose (if not always readily) what to feel, and with the two in creative combination we can choose how to act. As we learn to maintain a healthy relationship between our emotions and cognitions, we will be able to reduce pain, increase pleasure, and solve problems more easily.

I hope you have experienced some Arousal.

Notes to Part I

1 *Exogenous and endogenous arousal*: from a strictly constructivist viewpoint *all* 'exogenous' (externally originating) events are constructed 'endogenously' (internally).

2 *My curiosity and uncertainty.* In the domain of 'Meta-States' my meta-level of excitement and curiosity would be *about* my primary emotions of frustration and anxiety.

3 *Plato's passions and fears made it impossible for him to think.* It is not recorded whether Plato thought or felt that this was an emotional or a rational observation.

| AROUSAL | SENSATION | CONSTRUCTION | APPRAISAL | VOLITION |
| Part I | Part II | Part III | Part IV | Part V |

Part II SENSATION

Time after time as I listen to people talk about their feelings, I am struck by the wholly subjective and frequently overwhelming nature of their experience. As a therapist, I have seen too many clients at the mercy of their emotions, believing they had no choice but to give in to them. As a teacher, I have seen too many people who were emotionally not ready to learn, because they had only the foggiest notion of their emotional life and of the feelings of others.

Yet emotion is a kind of cognition as knowable as any other construct of the mind. In Part I, we discussed what happens before a feeling is felt (Arousal) and I invited the reader to begin to deconstruct this sequence of near-simultaneous events:

1. AROUSAL [external or internal input]
   leading to
2. SENSATION [unconscious physiological response and representation]
   leading to
3. CONSTRUCTION [unconscious connection to other bodymind effects: associative memory, past experience, present needs and values, etc.]
   leading to

4 APPRAISAL [(un)conscious cognitive assessment of events 1 - 3]
  leading to
5 VOLITION [the (un)conscious impulse to act]
  leading to
6 ACTION [the resulting behaviour]

Five events that happen in an instant leading to a sixth that may then seem inevitable. The result might be a flash of anger, an involuntary laugh, or an uncontrollable tear. Emotions are notoriously quick to move us. The word 'emotion' comes from the Latin *emovere*: to move, stir up, agitate.

Given the speed of these internal events (perhaps a fifth of a second from input to output), it's no wonder that we readily confuse our experience of one with our experience of the whole. It can get us into all sorts of trouble.

CONFUSION OF FEELING

Part II is about distinguishing the initial physiological events [*sensation*] from the bodymind associations [*construction*] and cognitions [*appraisal*] that follow, in order to better understand and deal with the whole schemozzle.

Why might we want to do this? Some people believe that feelings are best left to be felt rather than analyzed and that this makes for a richer experience of life. Yet if you believe that knowledge activates intelligence, and emotional intelligence is vital not just for survival but for furthering individual happiness and the human condition, do read on.

I shall invite you first to distinguish between *sensation* and *feeling*. Sensation can be defined as our mental representation of our physiological signalling systems; feeling as our mental cognizance, or processing, of the experience. If I stray from this sensation/feeling distinction on occasion, it is because, like most of us, I tend to use feeling words interchangeably. We don't have a great deal of choice. Our feeling-related experiences far outnumber our vocabulary for them, which means that our capacity for deconstructing emotional experience in order to better enjoy and employ it (one definition of 'emotional intelligence') is, shall we say, unpractised. We are still learning the language.

There is a lexicon of the principal terms – cognition, emotion, feeling, sensation, mood, and state – in Part I (page 10). Currently there is no consensus among neuroscientists and philosophers about what emotions 'are'. Antonio Damasio (see References and Further Reading) describes *emotions* as "basic bio-regulatory reactions," a collection of chemical and neural responses that play a regulatory role in our neurophysiology and constitute a substrate, or base, for *feelings*, which are our mental experience of the changes ensuing in body and brain. This may be a useful distinction for an academic studying the phenomena at cellular or microcircuit level to make, but here I shall use the terms emotion and feeling in their colloquial sense – interchangeably.

> WHAT ARE EMOTIONS/FEELINGS?
> They have been variously described as
> - bio-regulatory responses
> - remembered associations
> - carriers of multiple messages
> - positive or negative preferences
> - pleasurable or painful consciousness
> - a powerful manifestation of drives and instincts
> - an emergent property of information input and its unconscious associations[1]
> - a core component of our capacity for rational thought

Recognizing and describing our emotions helps shape the brain. Many of us find it very difficult to describe how we feel. We experience a confusion of internal sensations, associations, and evaluations. Or we experience a mix of emotions at the same time. Separating out and naming these is an essential skill in the building of identity. Parents who talk about feelings help their children learn who they are. Anger consultant Mike Fisher points out that "To know who I am, I need to know what I feel. When I know what I feel, I know who I am."

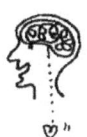

Our brains have the greatest difficulty separating what we feel from *how* we feel. The evidence for this comes from a half-century of neuropsychological research, which has produced a large number of scientific models describing how:

- We misremember events with an emotional component, yet because our 'memories' have produced specific pictures or sounds we are certain these events happened exactly that way.

- We imagine stimuli that are not present, yet because our emotion-influenced beliefs are based on them, we employ 'reason' to argue that they are present.

- We focus our attention on a limited number of stimuli, yet like to believe we have considered the whole event.

- We make decisions on the basis of incomplete information, yet readily assert that they are 'correct'.

- We make wild rushes to judgment about the motivation and behaviour of others, only to find later that we were – sometimes tragically – wrong.

EXERCISE IN SENSATION #1

I asked my emotionally highly articulate partner to distinguish, locate, name, and describe some of the strong sensations she feels. Here is her verbatim account ('C'), along with descriptions of similar feelings by other subjects ('K', 'Q', and 'S').

> The exercise is in two parts. You are invited to
>
> 1 Compare *your* experience of these emotions with the subjects' descriptions.
>
> 2 Separate the original *sensations* and their *location* from the *associations* and *interpretations* the subjects make around them.

'ANGER'

C A tightening in my solar plexus. Fire. Power that needs to lash out. If it doesn't lash out it boils away or knots. My jaw gets a restricting kind of feeling, constriction of the muscles before the lash out, tension that grabs in my stomach and jaw, even in my eyes, I can feel them grow, they're not relaxed. And it's very basic, primitive, it's got to do with protection, you're under threat, your ideas are being sabotaged, your will is undermined, there's an obstacle in your way and if you don't sort that out, it has to be sublimated and just festers.

K My voice gets louder, harder, sharper. My jaw becomes more fixed. Clenching. My internal organs are being squeezed. A sense of wanting to attack.

Q I feel neanderthal. I feel like my forehead and neck get smaller and shorter. My face gets rigid. I inflate my chest and don't let it go.

'EXCITEMENT' or 'JOY'

C ('Excitement') A bubbling feeling in the solar plexus, a fast feeling. It's got energy, it's dynamic, it moves so I want to take action, to be involved. It's a whole body thing. A sacral, sexual, faster, lighter feeling that includes all of myself, and I can feel my pulse get faster and my heart beats faster. I breathe faster. There's a lifting up of my eyebrows and my mouth. I'm ready to engage. And I want to move my whole body with excitement.

S ('Excitement') Constant waves, it's an all over thing. Almost a colour — yellow or red. A warm, rosy glow.

K ('Joy') Being able to breathe very clearly. A sort of tingling on the outside of my body. My muscles feel ready — I could spring up in the air. A sense inside like a gentle bubbling. And as the bubbles rise and break — ting — I want to skip.

'FEAR'

C Is in my chest. Like a restricting. You breathe in and hold your breath. It's a suspension. When I'm afraid, I stop, I don't breathe, in order to gauge the action I should take. This is survival stuff. You reduce your movement, reduce your sound. I can feel my eyes getting bigger to see the threat. I can feel my pupils getting bigger in order to assess it, and I'm ready to take action.

Q A tightening like a muscular tensing in my ribcage. I start to breathe higher in my chest, I have a sense of being stuck in the moment, and as my attention comes into my head I start thinking, "Oh god, what shall I do?" and I freeze and wait.

S My fear is of not being listened to and taken seriously, of not being valued. I feel it in my eyes. It's an observation of others' reactions. A thoughtfulness that distracts me from being confident. A sense of sinking in my chest. Breathlessness. Heaviness.

SENSATION AND EMOTION

There are similarities in the sample. Although subjects were asked to identify the *sensations* they experienced, they found it a challenge to distinguish these from the *constructions* and *appraisals* they related to their sensations (eg "This is survival stuff"). All identified the chest as the seat of 'Fear' and the whole body as the location of 'Joy'. Other similarities highlight anomalies: a "tightening" sensation and "faster" or "higher" breathing were linked to both 'Joy' and 'Fear', two very different emotions. And although we may suppose K's "clench" to be similar to C's "grab", it is apparent that the words represented quite different experiences of the 'Anger' both felt.

I asked my volunteers to identify the emotions they experienced routinely, supposing that a collective list of six or seven would emerge. In fact, they came up with varying lists of between five and twelve, and between them identified twenty-six different, diverse, and distinguishable feelings:

> 'Acceptance', 'Annoyance', 'Anger', 'Appreciation', 'Compassion', 'Confidence', 'Contentment', 'Creativity', 'Curiosity', 'Depression', 'Excitement', 'Fear', 'Frustration', 'Gratitude', 'Guilt', 'Happiness', 'Helplessness', 'Interest', 'Jealousy', 'Joy', 'Love', 'OK-ness', 'Pleasure', 'Resentment', 'Sadness', 'Shame'.

I am sure you will be able to add more of your own. We could argue the toss about which of these might be basic emotions and which might be variants or compounds, but it is clear to me now that however we separate out our feelings, it doesn't matter a jot what we call them or how many we have. The important thing is that they are uniquely ours. As we identify them, so they identify us.

Since Darwin (The Expression of Emotions in Man and Animals, 1872) first propounded a theory of universal emotions finding their expression in overt behaviour, researchers have attempted to generalize this area of subjective experience and reduce it to universal patterns.

> Tompkins (1962) and Izard (1977) proposed eight basic emotions, or "innate patterned responses controlled by hardwired brain systems." These were *Surprise, Interest, Joy, Rage, Fear, Disgust, Shame, Anguish.* Izard described *anxiety* as the combination of fear with any two from *guilt, interest, shame, anger, distress.*

Plutchik (1980) came up with a different eight: *Sadness, Disgust, Anger, Anticipation, Joy, Acceptance, Fear, Surprise*, which he arranged in eighths of a circle, proposing that further "non-basic, psychosocially derived, cognitively constructed, uniquely human emotions" would derive from a mix of adjacent eighths (eg *joy + acceptance = friendliness or love; fear + surprise = alarm*).

Panksepp (1982) used the behavioural consequences of the electrical stimulation of areas of rat brain to identify four basic emotions or "response patterns": *Panic, Rage, Fear, Expectancy*.

Expectancy is an interesting one, although in laboratory animals anticipating a further application of electricity that had earlier resulted in Panic, Rage, and Fear, it is much as you might expect.

Damasio (1994) proposed three varieties of feeling. (1) Five "universal" emotions: *Happiness, Sadness, Anger, Fear, Disgust*, which he called our "combined perception of certain bodily states with whatever thoughts they are juxtaposed to. (2) A number of variations fine-tuned by our individual experience of the five, which are "subtler shades of cognitive states connected to subtler variations of emotional body states," e.g. *Euphoria* and *Ecstasy* as variations on *Happiness*. (3) Minimal background feelings originating in the body alone, for example the feeling of *life*, or a sense of just *being*; states neither pleasant nor unpleasant.

Of course there are circumstances in which the ability to categorize – to extrapolate the general from the specific – as these researchers have done, can be useful. But when it comes to self-healing and learning, generalizing has its limitations. From a therapeutic point of view, it is the idiosyncrasy of the clients' subjective experience that defines them uniquely and is the key to them *changing* their subjective experience.

I compared the academics' findings with the experience of my volunteers. Only 'Anger' emerges as common to all, though 'Happiness' and 'Fear' come close. My subjects identified more variations of 'Happiness' ('Joy', 'Excitement', 'Love', 'Contentment', 'Gratitude', etc.) than the academics, but there was a near-consensus in the 'Anger' and 'Fear' categories. My volunteers didn't seem to have much time for 'Sadness'. This may be the company I keep, or it could be that they are all too busy finding things to be glad and mad about. One thing my research confirmed for me is the point about identity: the sum of our emotions is a summary of ourselves. You can check this out by compiling your own list. To what extent does it mirror who you are?

If what we feel is person-specific and no-one can agree on a collective list, what most modern theories have in common is agreement on the underlying structure of emotion: (1) Instigating Stimuli (AROUSAL); (2) Physiological Correlates (SENSATION); (3) Physical Coherence (CONSTRUCTION); (4) Cognitive Evaluation (APPRAISAL); and (5) Motivational Impulse (VOLITION).

EXERCISE IN SENSATION #2

> 1 What sensations are you aware of at the moment? Try not to interpret what you are experiencing. Locate and label the direct physiological stimuli that you sense and do your best to describe them in sensory-specific language. What is your body awareness?
>
> 2 Consider what *associations* you have to these sensations.
>
> 3 What do these sensations and their associations *'mean'* to you?

I can, with some difficulty, distinguish these three levels of internal processing: sensation, association, and meaning.

1 Physical sensations. A sense of the weight of my body in the chair, of my hands moving as I type, some kind of slight gnawing in my stomach, a crick in one side of the neck, and an unsettled sense, difficult to locate and describe, that is probably in my head, heart, and gut. (Not all in sensory-specific language, you will note, but I'm doing my best.)

2 Bodymind associations and constructions. I'm convinced that the "gnawing" is the onset of hunger, a familiar association. The "crick" I link to poor posture. The "unsettled" to some kind of feeling of restlessness and uncertainty.

3 Mind evaluations and appraisals of meaning. The idea of hunger induces 'anxiety' (when am I going to eat?). The idea of poor posture brings further anxiety, this time about health

and fitness, so I experience the crick as an 'ache'. I evaluate restlessness and uncertainty in terms of the 'curiosity' and 'excitement' I feel about what I am learning, and also to what I recognize as 'annoyance' at the noises other people are making nearby as they prepare to go out. This prompts feelings of 'guilt', followed by 'love' and 'appreciation', as I am reminded of the needs of those making the noises (my wife and son) and of the benefits that accrue to me from my relationships with them.

Even in my present relatively neutral emotional state it is evident there is a lot going on in there. No wonder that it can feel like a confusion of events when things are really shaken or stirred.

SENSATION AND CONSTRUCTION

My anxiety, curiosity, and guilt are thoughts as much as feelings. I shall have more to say about how the mind conflates these stages of construction and appraisal in Parts III and IV. Meanwhile, how can we be certain that feelings are constructs of the mind? Even a neck-ache? Isn't pain a purely physical phenomenon?

Well, no. If I compare the ache in my neck with a similar ache in my legs after a long walk, I am aware of an entirely different experience. I evaluate the first as 'unhealthy', because I associate it with poor posture, and the second as 'healthy', because I associate it with enjoyable exercise. So I experience the unhealthy sensation in my neck as 'painful' (prompting an emotion of 'anxiety'), and the healthy sensation in my legs as 'pleasurable' (prompting an emotion of 'happiness').

If such similar sensations can engender emotions as radically dissimilar as anxiety and happiness, it can only be because my associations with, and appraisals of, the sensations – my unconscious and conscious thoughts about them – have become the sensations themselves. Anxiety is inextricably associated with my aching neck, happiness with my aching legs.

Emotions are, in fact, just another form of cognition. If you would like a detailed appraisal of evolutionarily determined emotional processing compared to cognitive processing or "mere thoughts," as he puts it, see Daniel Goleman's Emotional Intelligence (1996).

SENSATION AND METAPHOR

In the research examples on pages 22-23, you will have noticed something about the language subjects used to describe their sensations. Similes, analogies, and figures of speech popped up everywhere. In describing my own body awareness (pages 26-27), I tried to stick to neutral language, but still couldn't help using words like "gnawing", "crick", "unsettled". Metaphors like these – and the "bubbling", "boils", "waves", and "knots" of others – are signposts to the larger landscape of unconscious experience. Less obvious, but just as metaphorical, are C's "restricting", "an obstacle in your way," and "it moves so I want to take action." We have even seen that the simple words we use for emotions themselves – 'Sadness', 'Anger', 'Joy' – are not simple at all, but omnibus terms carrying a variety of subjective experience.

EMOTION AS METAPHOR

Metaphor (Greek *meta* = beyond + *phora* = carrier) is a higher order container with the capacity for holding a great deal more emotional experience than an impartial description of their related sensations. Indeed, it may be impossible to talk about feelings in any depth without moving into metaphor. As we attempt to sort through the confusion of bodymind events, it is as if our minds have to ask themselves: what in my unconscious is this experience *like*?

Given that we have many more emotional experiences than speakable descriptions for them, we have little choice but to fish around in the depths of our unconscious for recognizable, isomorphic (alike-structure) constructs that already exist. Metaphor is the first language of feeling, a carrier of multiple messages from the otherwise unspeakably deep levels of subjective experience. 'Happy as a lark.' 'Scared stiff.' 'Down in the dumps.'

"We not only describe our feelings in metaphor," say psychotherapists James Lawley and Penny Tompkins, "we think and make sense of them through metaphor, and we behave in ways that are consistent with our metaphors."

A feeling of 'depression' may be very difficult for a client to discuss analytically or conceptually with a counsellor. But what happens if the counsellor questions the client in a different kind of way?

> And whereabouts is 'depression'?
> *Behind my forehead and about an inch in.*
>
> And 'depression' behind your forehead and about an inch in is like what?
> *It's like a great wave of blackness.*
>
> What kind of blackness?
> *The sort from a night sky at sea without stars. If I could find one star it would be less intense.*

And can you find one star?
When I do, I'll see light at the end of the tunnel.

And what kind of light could that light be?

And so on. Every feeling will have a location in the metaphor landscape that exists within and around us. It will be 'like' something. And both its likeness and location will be ways into communicating with it.

Even if we talk in shared metaphor, we are never walking in the same landscape. 'Light at the end of the tunnel' is a phrase I have heard clients use countless times, but when questioned cleanly, without any assumptions, every client's 'tunnel', 'light', and 'end' turned out to be different to every other client's. Every configuration of the symbols that made up their metaphors was different. Every placing and sequencing of the symbols in time and space was unique.

This particularity of information and perception has clear implications for the way facilitators orchestrate the facilitative experience. As we minimize our contagion of the client's internal process with our personal associations, interpretations, and suggestions, we encourage the individual's capacities for self-learning, healing, and growth.

FACILITATING METAPHOR

I'm feeling down in the dumps.
And you're feeling down in the dumps. And when you're feeling down in the dumps, what kind of dumps is that dumps you are down in?

It's like a hole full of rubbish.
And a hole full of rubbish. And when a hole full of rubbish, where could that rubbish come from?

Other people throwing it in.
And other people throwing it in. And when other people throwing it in, what kind of other people?

People I'm scared of, and I let them dump their rubbish on me.
And people you're scared of, and you let them dump their rubbish on you. And when you let people you're scared of dump their rubbish on you, what happens next?

I know they're only dumping it on me because I just happen to be already in the dump, so I realize I have to climb out.

And you realize you have to climb out. And when you realize you have to climb out, what happens next?

Clean questioning does not address the client directly. It addresses the information that comes up for the client, particularly information encoded in autogenic (self-generated) metaphor. The meaning will be released as the client gets to know more about how they have constructed this unique, underlying, and otherwise unspeakable representation of feeling.

EXERCISE IN SENSATION #3

> 1 Identify one or two of your key emotions. Name them what you will.
>
> 2 Separate as far as you can the related sensations from your subsequent constructions and appraisals.
>
> 3 What *other associations* can you make to these same sensations?
>
> 4 Imagine having the sensations *without* the associations. What would it be like to think, 'Oh, that's a heaviness in the gut, or a lightness in the heart ... full stop'?

A detailed blueprint for the construction of emotion is drawn up in Part III. Meanwhile, a reminder: emotions don't just happen.

Note to Part II

1 *A feeling as an 'emergent property' of the bodymind system*: for more on emergence see powersofsix.com, articles at wayfinderpress.co.uk, and the book The Power of Six.

| AROUSAL | SENSATION | CONSTRUCTION | APPRAISAL | VOLITION |
| Part I | Part II | Part III | Part IV | Part V |

Part III CONSTRUCTION

Je pense, donc je suis. I think, therefore I am. Descartes (1637)
We are, and then we think. Damasio (1994)

EMOTIONS DON'T JUST HAPPEN

If I were to ask you to spend a few moments thinking of your lover ... your gas bill ... and a swarm of killer bees ... it is likely that you would undergo a range of imperceptible but nonetheless measurable physiological changes to your breathing, heart rate, and galvanic skin response that would relate to a variety of emotions, from joy to alarm, and all within a very short space of time. This is remarkable, because I only invited you to think about these things, not to have any feelings about them. What then is the sameness of feeling and thinking, emotion and cognition, and what are the differences between them?

The answers lie in the way our brains *construct* experience, and this is what Part III is about. Emotions, cognitions, beliefs, and imaginings don't just come into being out of the blue. Nor do they originate in consciousness, as many people suppose. My fond hope is that the more we get to know about the way these largely unconscious events are created, the better we will be able to understand, adjust, and enjoy our emotional responses, enhance our emotional intelligence, and facilitate others to understand, enjoy, and enhance theirs.

EMOTIONAL CONDITIONING
The brain is the body's captive audience. Antonio Damasio

Children who experience repeated reminders of their worth tend to grow up feeling secure in themselves. Reiteration changes the brain, as those who practise NLP anchoring for state control will know. And the intensity of the experience reinforces the change. Those who undergo repeated physical, sexual, or mental abuse as children can suffer a similar kind of brain damage to victims of accidents or the trauma of war. If the pre-frontal lobes associated with motivation, judgment, and impulse control have developed abnormally through traumatic experience, even a minor event can trigger massive reactions of violence, anger, or phobia.

The trauma does not have to be direct or even discernible. As neuroscientist Ian Robertson writes in Mind Sculpture:

> *In brains already programmed for prejudice, the circuits can be strengthened further by every massacre, every conflict over housing or land, [every] mass media promotion of stereotypes ... whole political systems are constructed to shape the most primitive emotional reactions in the brains of their constituents.*

I anticipate a time when it is everyone's social responsibility to understand how this kind of psychological and political conditioning can happen. Conditioned responses are a consequence of our need to adapt to severe circumstance, but they are also a fact of everyday life. You could say that all our emotions are conditioned by evolution, observation, and social interaction. It's just that some of them give us more problems than others.

Part III has three sections applicable to the construction of every kind of feeling:

>   Novel and Conditioned
>   Direct and Indirect
>   Felt and Interpreted

NOVEL AND CONDITIONED FEELINGS

The sensory inputs that come to us every moment of our lives include novel stimuli from external events – what Goleman calls "raw physical signals" – and conditioned stimuli from internal events.[1]

When Pavlov's dog first heard the bell, the stimulus was novel and *un*conditioned. As the dog learned to associate the bell with the appearance of food, the sound created a conditioned stimulus that itself would prompt the salivating response.

	THE CONSTRUCTION OF EMOTION	
Stage 1	*process*	*neural pathways*
Arousal	Input from external 'novel stimuli' and internal 'conditioned stimuli'…	↓↓↓↓↓↓↓
	Somatosensory reception by visual, auditory, kinesthetic (external and internal), olfactory and gustatory receptor systems …	

Sensory receptors translate this input into the language of the brain and transmit their signals to a complex two-lobe inner structure of the brain called the *thalamus* (Greek 'inner chamber').

	Stage 2	*process*	*neural pathways*
	Sensation	Signals from sensory receptors feed directly to the thalamic 'relay centre' …	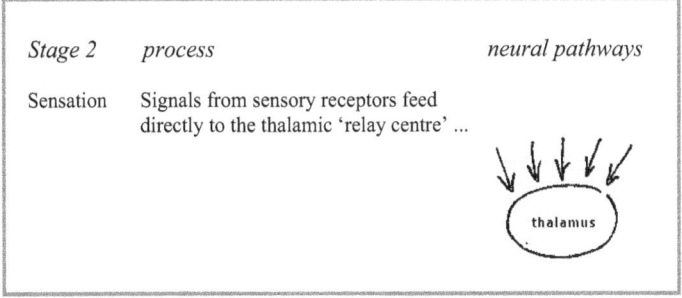

So far, so straightforward. Now comes the remarkable part.

DIRECT AND INDIRECT FEELINGS

Our knowledge of what happens next has been revolutionized by neuroscientist Joseph LeDoux's research, which has considerable implications for psychotherapy, counselling, and every kind of human facilitation. LeDoux was the first to reveal the means by which the thalamus, acting as a kind of relay centre, releases *two sets* of sensory projections:

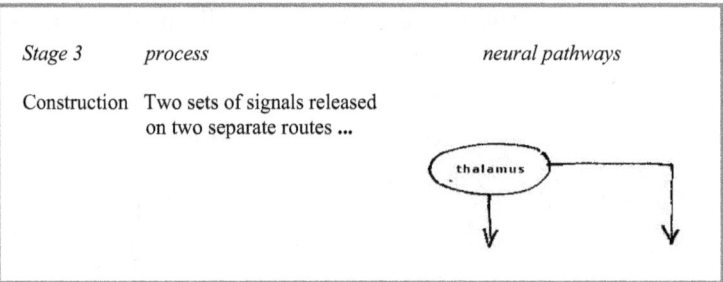

Stage 3   *process*   *neural pathways*

Construction   Two sets of signals released on two separate routes ...

Although each step on the neural pathway is represented here as having a linear connection to the next, this is in fact a systemic, recursive process. The various parts of the brain are not just involved once, but are re-involved throughout. 'Pathway', 'step', etc. are my metaphors.

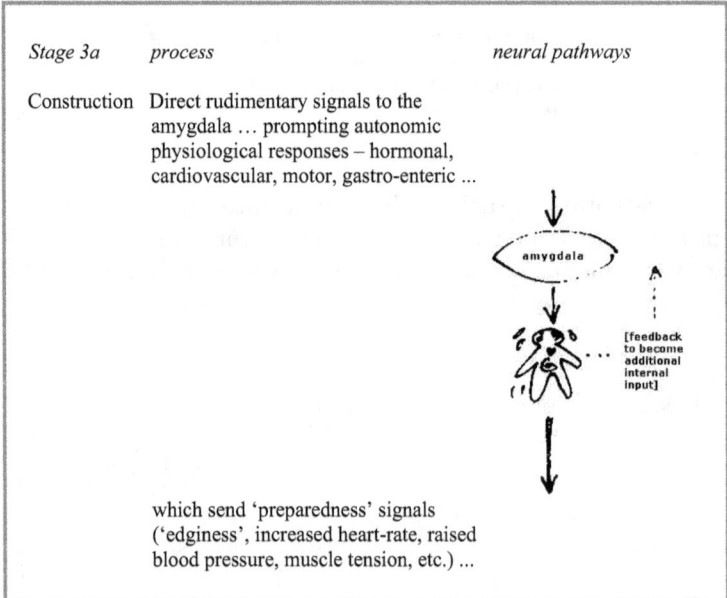

Stage 3a   *process*   *neural pathways*

Construction   Direct rudimentary signals to the amygdala ... prompting autonomic physiological responses – hormonal, cardiovascular, motor, gastro-enteric ...

[feedback to become additional internal input]

which send 'preparedness' signals ('edginess', increased heart-rate, raised blood pressure, muscle tension, etc.) ...

The first set of signals takes a fast track from the thalamus direct to the *amygdala* (Greek 'almond'), the brain's 'emotional processor', where they arrive *before* the second set of signals finds its way to the neo-cortex, or 'thinking brain'. The working of the almond-shaped mass of neurons in the temporal lobes, more properly known as the amygdaloid complex (there is one amygdala in each hemisphere), means that emotional responses must always begin to manifest *before* the higher brain centres involved in thinking, reasoning, and consciousness can be engaged. To put it another way, *we feel before we think*.

The direct route, according to LeDoux's research, requires the 'preparedness' signals to cross only a single synapse, which may be the reason they cannot support fine distinctions. Our first glimpse of a twisted shape on the ground may prompt physiological reactions to 'snake', but a moment later, having scrolled through the cortical options, we are able to see 'dead twig'. Signals from the olfactory receptors ('smell') are a special case. Their survival role in determining what was edible or toxic, allowing food that had led to sickness to be avoided another time, gives them a direct route to the cerebral cortex.

The amygdala has been called the storehouse of old brain / archetypal / innate memory and its early warning system prepares the body to respond via a rudimentary representation of the incoming stimuli before we fully know what we are responding to. This pre-empts the need for thinking *what* to do, when any time saved could make the difference between life and death.

> *Under the coarse logic of evolutionary survival, danger should not have to be constantly relearned. Once bitten, twice shy.* Ian Robertson

It takes about seven milliseconds for these elementary signals to transmit to the thalamus and a few milliseconds more for the thalamus to relay them to the amygdala. Only a few thousandths of a second – less than a blink – for our bodies to begin to react to that rustle in the grass as if it were a predator.

Every millisecond of our lives, our physical and mental state is in flux as we adapt to the world. We relax or tense. Our heart rate, breathing, blood pressure, perspiration response, and a dozen other physiological measures change – activity that mirrors fleeting shifts in the balance of alerting and quietening neurotransmitters in the brain. Normally, only the more extreme of these instinctive responses will be noticeable, but many of the subtler 'micro-emotions' that flit across the face or are expressed by the involuntary twitch of a muscle in a finger or a foot can be tracked by a trained facilitator in the split second immediately after a question has been asked (often before the question has been completed) and just before it has been fully appraised by the client.

> *The movements of expression ... reveal the thoughts and intentions of others more truly than do words.*   Charles Darwin

Though one may have to look carefully. In 1980, social psychologist Paul Ekman videoed Japanese subjects watching an emotionally arousing film in the knowledge that they were being recorded. Their expressions hardly varied. In fact, slow-motion analysis of the videotape showed that their smiles and polite expressions had been superimposed on *fleeting, prior-occurring facial movements*. These, reckoned Ekman, were their basic emotions "leaking through".

> In NLP, the perception of subtle physiological distinctions is called 'sensory acuity', though the phrase is often used loosely and may have lost some of its original precision. 'Calibration' is noticing patterns to these distinctions over time in a particular individual. It may be possible for amygdala-biased signals to reach *and prime* the cerebral cortex before it receives its neutral thalamic set. If so, this would put notions of the purity of 'rational thought' even further into question.

As basic fast-track signals are relayed to the amygdala, a more complete set is being transmitted to the sensory cortices and the neo-cortex (new-brain/explicit memory) for cerebral processing.

Stage 3b	process	neural pathways
Construction	Indirect fuller signals relayed from the thalamus to create neural codings of the stimuli in the sensory cortices ...	
		From sensory cortices ...
		to 'memory' [conflation of past events and feelings; pre- existing associations, conditioned responses, present beliefs, values, attitudes, needs, goals] ...
	Thalamic signals processed in memory: are the signals familiar? what do they relate to / link to / prompt? ...	
	Releasing 'significance hypothesis' signals – could be this, could be that ...	

Every neural circuit adds time. It takes this cortical set of signals significantly longer – perhaps twenty milliseconds – to find its way through the cerebral cortex to prompt the higher-level reasoning which reminds us that the rustle we heard in the grass might not be a predator but the wind.

By a trick of perception – spot the milliseconds difference – the shorter emotional trip and the longer cognitive trip will seem to be synchronized. We wake feeling tense, heart thumping, before we know what caused that bump in the night, yet the conviction that an intruder entered the room or the cat fell off the mantelpiece may already be present as we wake. Conditioned fears produce conditioned responses. Repeated life events produce conditioned responses. Indeed, conditioned learning can occur after a single unconditioned stimulus / response pairing if the pairing is strong enough.

Ian Robertson describes experiments in which photographs of faces were presented to volunteers at the same time as an unpleasant noise. The faces were later re-presented silently and subliminally (so quickly that they could not be seen consciously), and brain-scan imaging indicated activity in the amygdala every time. The inescapable conclusion was that *the emotional centres of the subjects' brains were reacting to unpleasant associations from the past of which their conscious minds remained unaware.* Scientific confirmation of a phenomenon that psychotherapists see at work every week.

Robertson's subliminal experiments involved subjects who had access to very recent explicit memory that would have been relatively untainted. Most of our recollections are in fact easily corrupted in the process of associating contemporary goals, beliefs, and needs to past behaviours, emotions, and events. Memory is always a variable reconstruction; never an instant replay.

One of David Grove's great contributions to the practice of facilitating others has been in teaching us how to work with symbolic, rather than cognitive, recollection and to treat all client information as a metaphor for what is really going on in the unconscious. Metaphor, as Grove said, mediates the interface between the conscious and unconscious mind.[2]

During the appraisal stage of the construction process, cerebral 'significance' signals are assessed *in combination with* physiological 'preparedness' signals ...

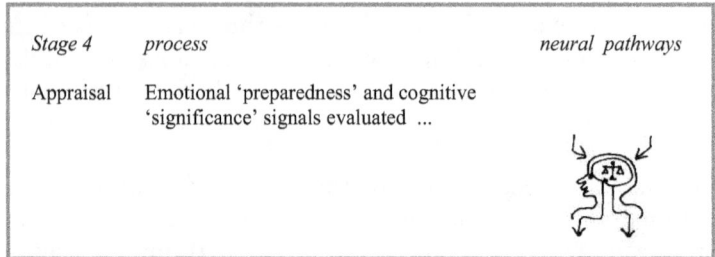

... and what emerges is neither an emotion nor a cognition, but both in combination: a product of the continuous monitoring of the body during the cognitive process *incorporated into* the continuous monitoring of the brain during the emotional process. An emocognition or feeling-thought is the result. So much for our romantic myths of 'abstract' thought and 'pure' feeling. Damasio describes the organism interacting with the environment as an ensemble and the interaction being neither of the body alone nor of the brain alone. The mind is embodied as much as the body is embrained.[3]

FELT AND INTERPRETED FEELINGS

Volition – the impulse to act on our emotions – derives from the resulting 'felt preferences' (pleasant or unpleasant) and 'action preferences' (towards or away from) combining with and influencing each other. Faintly or noticeably, but without exception rapidly, our bodies react to events with an orienting or defensive reflex, and with 'lighter' or 'heavier' sensations.

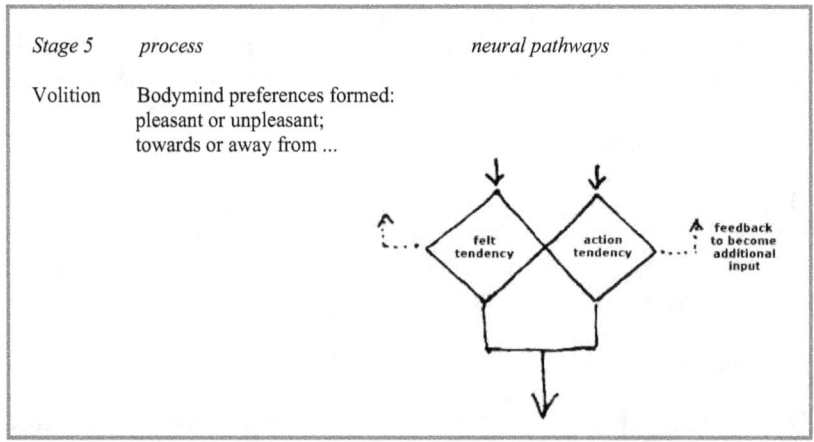

These twin volitional signals feed back to the sensory cortices proprioceptively (internally produced and received) to become further input for the bodymind as it primes itself to take action. Only a microsecond later will we interpret and label the experience as a whole, stages 1 to 5, as 'joy', 'fear', 'anger' and so on.

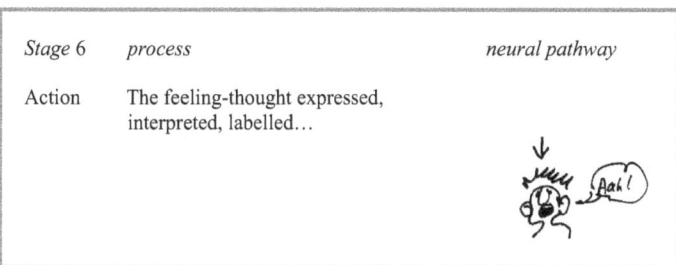

Stage 6	process	neural pathway
Action	The feeling-thought expressed, interpreted, labelled…	

CHANGING FEELINGS

Emotions are not immutable. Unpleasant emotions do not have to be disabling. In the instant after volition (stage 5) and before action (stage 6), the structure provides us with a moment of choice. The moment may not always be well defined, but it does exist, and like any other moment in the process, it can be expanded, explored, and mapped in a variety of ways using Clean techniques.[4]

In Part II of this paper, I proposed that the sum of our feelings is a summary of ourselves. Change any stage of a feeling and you change yourself.

We have seen that amygdala and cerebral cortex are interactive parts of the same neurological system, yet it is a physical reality of the brain that there are many more connections from the amygdala to the cortex than there are the other way round. No single fact about our neurophysiology, says Robertson, is more relevant to explaining war, conflict, and environmental recklessness in the human race. While it is certainly possible for the higher brain centres to influence the wilder excesses of our feelings, it often takes a heck of an effort to keep reason afloat.

LeDoux suggests that this asymmetry between amygdala and cortex means that the process of conventional psychoanalysis will always be a prolonged one, because the aim of psychoanalysis is for the cortex to gain control over the amygdala. The problem is the same for all models of counselling and coaching that depend on the primacy of conscious cognition over unconscious emotional processes. At the mental health charity Mind, I worked with several cognitively unsophisticated clients who had been rejected for psychoanalytic and cognitive-behavioural therapy because they had been assessed as having insufficient insight into themselves. Yet they responded readily to Clean questioning, because it supported them to self-model at whatever level of emotive or cognitive constructs they were able, or chose, to access.

CASE HISTORY: JANET

56-year old Janet's first words to me were, "I feel worn out since my mother died and I don't want to die before my 57th birthday." In order to feel better she needed "someone to talk to, a tidier house and being able to dance again." To dance again, her "feet needed to feel better."

In the following transcript, the full Clean Language syntax[4] has been condensed.

> And what kind of feet are those feet that need to feel better?
> *They're worried feet.*
>
> And what kind of feet were those feet before they were worried?
> *They used to dance a lot.*
>
> And where could feet that used to dance a lot come from?
> *I must have got them from my mother and father, they liked dancing and walking.*
>
> And where could a mother and father who liked dancing and walking come from?
> *We used to go on holidays at the Holiday Fellowship.*
>
> And where could Holiday Fellowship come from?
> *From God.*
>
> What kind of God?
> *A caring God.*
>
> And that's a caring God like what?
> *Like my cat.*
>
> And what kind of cat is my cat?
> [Visibly softens] *Very nice. Very relaxed. I love it.*
>
> And would very nice very relaxed I love it cat be interested in going to worried feet?
> [Smiles] *Maybe.* [One foot starts to rub against the other]
>
> And what happens when very nice cat goes to worried feet?
> *It massages it.*
>
> And when it massages it then what happens?
> *I'm doing it to myself.*

And then what happens?
My feet feel better.

Clean questioning helped Janet model her feelings, thoughts, and beliefs as symbolic constructs ("worried feet," "caring God like my cat," etc.), allowing her to access and explore them at the levels of unconscious Sensation and Construction without the need for cognitive Appraisal.

Next we consider the penultimate stage of the structure of emocognition, appraisal, and inquire further into the workings of what we have no choice but to use for the purpose: our unique and original, tangled and extravagant, ingenious and amazing brains.

Notes to Part III

1 *'External' and 'internal' events:* I use the words here in the sense of our perception of events as originating outside or inside the body. Our *representation* of events, whatever their origin, is by this definition 'internal'. For the system as a whole, of course, space is neither 'external' nor 'internal'.

2 *Metaphor mediates between the conscious and unconscious mind*: for examples of this in action, see the client/facilitator exchanges on pages 40 (Janet), 50 (Clare), and 63 (Ben).

3 *The mind is embodied as much as the body is embrained.* Susan Greenfield in The Private Life of the Brain (2001) argues that it is the *iteration* between body and brain – their function in concert – that generates (is) consciousness itself.

4 *Clean techniques, Clean Language syntax, etc.*: for more see cleanlanguage.co.uk, powersofsix.com, and the books Metaphors in Mind (2000), Clean Language (2008), The Power of Six (2009), and Trust Me, I'm The Patient (2012).

| AROUSAL | SENSATION | CONSTRUCTION | APPRAISAL | VOLITION |
| Part I | Part II | Part III | Part IV | Part V |

Part IV APPRAISAL

Love is ... an emocognition.

A woman drops her purse in the High Street and stoops to pick it up. Following behind her is a young man. He stops, not to help her, not to steal her purse, but to slap her bottom. It is an impulsive act. He is immediately contrite. For most people the thought of slapping the woman's bottom, had it occurred at all, would have been a passing fragment of a thought among the hundreds that flit through the brain every moment. There would have been little chance of it being put into action, because the feeling that prompted it would have been appraised, and any desire to act on it suppressed, in a fraction of a second. But a few months ago, the young man was the passenger in a car driven by a drunken friend and there was an impact accident in which the frontal lobes of his brain were damaged.

There have been countless studies of victims of this kind of injury which show it leading to radical personality change, typically from thoughtful and mature to impulsive and erratic. When the frontal lobe networks responsible for judgment and impulse control are disrupted, it is the *appraisal* stage of emocognitive processing that is most affected.

Part IV has three sections:

> *Feelings Tell Us How We Are Doing*
> Conscious and unconscious appraisal. The more understanding we have of the unconscious part, the better we will be able to manage the conscious part.
>
> *Reason Is Nowhere Pure*
> An analysis of the crucial components of appraisal – the involvement and make-up of memory, and the importance of personal belief systems.
>
> *Fear Has The Largest Eyes Of All*
> How appraisal fits into the brain's construction of the core emotion in psychopathology, fear.

FEELINGS TELL US HOW WE ARE DOING

Give the co-founders of NLP, Bandler and Grinder, their due: they were thirty years ahead of their time in pointing out that all experience is constructed unconsciously. Neuroscience has proven it to be so many times in the last thirty years, yet we are still having to remind ourselves.

Appraisal is the fourth of the five stages in the construction of emocognition and one of the most sophisticated, convoluted, and potentially misleading functions of the human brain. I used to think of appraisal as a purely rational activity – I experienced an emotion one way, then looked at it objectively in another – but pure intellect and pure emotion are what philosopher-scientist Alfred Korzybski called structural fictions: they do not exist. They are inextricably mixed in the crucible of the unconscious.

I shall generally refer to the unconscious, or pre-conscious, stages of the process as *Appraisal*, and to the conscious stage as *Reappraisal*. When both are in accord, all is well. When they contradict, as they often do, there will be conflict. Biologist Paul Griffiths describes two levels of appraisal:

> *Low-level evaluation of perceptual inputs driven only by simple features of the situation detected early in perceptual processing and relative to an urgent interpretation of the situation.*[1]

I take this to be Damasio's 'low road' of sensory signalling, which I referred to in Part III as the direct amygdala path. And:

Higher level later evaluation that is relative to the non-urgent multiple concerns of the organism.

Damasio's 'high road', or the indirect cortical path. Higher level later evaluation takes place both consciously and pre-consciously – that is, out of awareness – but is available to consciousness on reflection. This would give each appraisal event three inter-related phases:

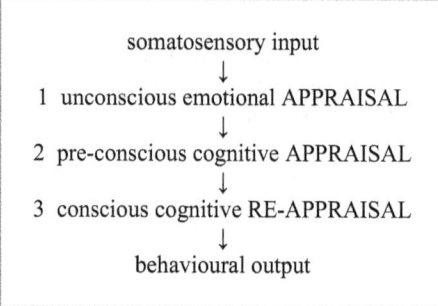

Phases of Appraisal

Systems like this are anything but linear, of course. The phases do not simply start at the top of the diagram and stop at the bottom. There is direct emotional input into the re-appraisal phase that prevents it going on forever (see Hamlet and The Recursivity Syndrome on page 45), while some of the results of re-appraisal feed back to influence the earlier phases and in turn become further input. It is a systemic, recursive loop. The process is pretty much the same, but each loop has slightly different input and output.

We will concentrate here on the non-conscious phases of appraisal, as the brain receives the body's proprioceptive 'physiological readiness' signals – *the direct path* ... assesses them in combination with the mind's cerebrally processed 'significance' signals that add idiosyncratic meaning to feeling – *the indirect path* ... to produce the mix of 'felt' and 'action' tendencies that make up our sense of volition, the impulse to act (stage 5, page 38).

As we saw in Part III, this is a byzantine journey. In a split second, the brain may receive billions of these signals activating many millions of neurons generating millions of firing patterns over a huge number of circuits across a variety of brain regions in a multi-associative process predisposed by genes and conditioned by life events. No wonder we generalize, delete, and distort so much as we process this onslaught, and so often get it wrong.

> ## To Be or Not To Be: Hamlet and the Recursivity Syndrome
>
> Re-appraisal is the conscious evaluation of what might be the outcome of acting on our emocognitions. The nightmare of the 'rational' mind is attempting to evaluate the outcome of the outcome of the outcome in endless regress. Only an emotion can limit the limitless range of plausible consequences that would otherwise have to be considered before any decision to act. Even allowing the throw of a die to decide would depend on the emotion-influenced options assigned to the numbers and the emotion-inspired will to act on the result. What finally motivated Hamlet out of analysis into action was his desire for revenge (resulting in murder and mayhem, unfortunately). Emotion and motivation have the same Latin root: *movere*, to move. Emotions move us. This leads not only to the impulse to act, but also to an opportunity for re-appraisal. These final stages in the construction of emocognition are considered in Part V, Volition.

Feelings get us into appraisal. We can now see that feelings get us out of appraisal; indeed, feelings depend on appraisal.

> Here is my secret. It is very simple. I see with my heart.
> (*Voici mon secret. Il est très simple. On ne voit bien qu'avec mon cœur.*)
>
> Antoine de Saint-Exupéry

The interval between events in the brain and our awareness of them in the bodymind is very short indeed – nowhere near long enough for us to separate our awareness of its structural stages (Arousal → Sensation → Construction → Appraisal) without rigorous training and practice. Whether you experience a rollercoaster ride as joyful or dreadful will depend on how you evaluate your expectations of the ride with your feelings about who may be accompanying you, your need (or not) for control, and your judgment of the serious discrepancies between your experience of balance on the ground and balance in the air. Love it or hate it?

Only after your feelings have been through five stages of construction, including three phases of appraisal, will you know! [2]

REASON IS NOWHERE PURE

Our brains have evolved to experience an endless succession of (re)constructions of past events, pre-existing associations, and conditioned responses in combination with present-day (that is, 'remembered present') beliefs, values, attitudes, needs, and goals. It is this medley, this kettle of fish, this wild inextricable maze that we call 'memory'. It is in no one place in the brain, but distributed throughout in what Damasio calls "dispositional representations" or "dormant firing potentialities."

Memory is a live event. It is not a recording. It is happening while we are riding roller-coasters as much as it is while taking exams or baking bread. Anything may prompt it and it is intrinsic to the appraisal process.

Belief and value systems have a pivotal importance in memory and an incalculable influence on appraisal. The philosopher A.C. Grayling suggests that almost all our emotions involve beliefs and values, or what some researchers call 'value structures' – the memory's cluster of norms, goals, values, and preferences. If we feel shame, says Grayling, it is because we believe we have done something that deserves contempt. If we feel compassion, it is because we believe that the object of our sympathy is suffering in a way that merits our concern. Our belief and value structures are predisposing our feelings.

Appraise comes from the Old French *prisier*, to price, evaluate from the Old French *value*, meaning worth. When we appraise or evaluate our sensations, we are simply pricing their worth to us. It is not too difficult to appraise the worth of a pleasant feeling, but where is the value in a painful feeling?

APPRAISING VALUES

burning building → fear → I get out = value (of survival)
fulfilled in positive action

I lie → anxiety → I feel guilty = value (of honesty)
honoured in pain of denial

A person with a problem around forgiveness, say, might invest the value of compassion in another while denying it in themself. The value is held by the person in the painful feeling that attends its denial.

FEAR HAS THE LARGEST EYES OF ALL

Those who suffer 'high anxiety', 'phobia', 'obsessive-compulsive disorder,' 'panic attacks,' or 'post-traumatic stress' – or any one of a host of other conditions involving the fear response – are honouring the value of survival of the organism in the face of perceived threat.

Those single inverted commas mark the neurolinguistic trap that lies in wait for all facilitators and health professionals – that of inadvertently contaminating the client's distinctive description of their actual symptoms with our schematic second-hand labels. 'Phobia', 'panic attack,' etc. are handy containers for sorting the enormous miscellany of subjective states that have their common origin in fear, but applying a generic label to an individual condition, even once, may affect the individual's beliefs about themselves for evermore. Manifestations of the fear response will usually have a pattern to their context, their cause, or their construction, but the particulars of the pattern will be unique to each sufferer.

LeDoux suggests a theory of panic attacks based on internal signals of heightened bodily arousal prompting the memory-inspired *belief* that a panic attack is occurring. The belief is likely to be reinforced by a further belief in 'panic' as an abnormal state beyond one's control and a belief in 'attack' as an unwarranted event of external origin – all contributing to an unconscious appraisal that what is occurring or about to occur is unsolicited, inevitable, and probably unmanageable.

Interestingly, the word *panic* derives from *Pan,* the otherwise benign Greek god of the woods, whose sudden appearances were said to cause irrational fear. The sight of a snake or a spider, the feeling of an enclosed space with no escape route, a sudden loud noise – almost anything provided it has been linked to a traumatic or life-threatening episode in the biographical or ancestral past – may trigger reactions that are more than a match for any present-day reasoned re-appraisal of the actual threat.

How then is the fear response constructed and what clues may it contain in helping to assess places for intervention, or in facilitating the client to self-model?

The Neurophysiology Of Fear

Stage	process	example
1 AROUSAL	Input from life events	spider appears
	Somatosensory reception: visual signals received …	see spider
2 SENSATION	Signals from sensory receptors direct to thalamic 'relay centre' …	
3 CONSTRUCTION	Which releases two sets of signals …	
3a	Rudimentary 'fast-track' direct to the amygdala for emotional processing … Prompting autonomic physiological responses, which feed back as additional sensory input to Stage 1 as 'preparedness' arousal signals …	
3b	Meanwhile fuller 'slow-track' signals from thalamus to sensory cortices and cerebral cortex are connecting to 'memory' (past and pre-existing associations, events, feelings; conditioned responses; present beliefs, values, needs, attitudes, goals) …	
	Connecting to e.g. childhood memory of a carer's negative reaction to spider or to another related trauma, or to idea that spiders can be okay …	
	Prompting 'meaning/significance' signals …	
4 APPRAISAL	Fast 'preparedness' and slower 'significance' signals evaluated for their relative potential … At same time as bodymind preferences are formed: unpleasant/pleasant, away from/toward …	
	Resulting in the feeling-thought being labelled internally, e.g., *I have a phobia about spiders!'* ('remembered association' or 'conditioned response')	
5 VOLITION	Impulse to act on 'phobic response'	desire to fight, flee, or freeze
6 ACTION	Behaviour / languaging …	confront: *"lash out"* escape: *" get away"* or do nothing: *"scared stiff"*
	State eventually returns to normal …	until the next time

Each stage of the process may be extremely difficult to distinguish from the rest in the normal run of events, but is readily accessible with Clean questioning.

CASE HISTORY: CLARE

Clare is in her late twenties. For twelve years, she has been suffering from what she has learnt to call panic attacks. Her doctor has prescribed anti-depressants, which lighten her mood a little, but haven't stalled the 'attacks' or improved her self-confidence.

The Clean Language syntax of the facilitator has been condensed.

> *I can't understand what's happening, because my mind is telling me I'm perfectly ok.*
> And when you can't understand what's happening and your mind is telling you you're perfectly ok, what would you like to have happen?
>
> *I want to sort my head out, I want to feel normal.*

We spend some time developing this outcome: What kind of 'sort'? Is there anything else about 'normal'? etc. Then:

> And what happens just before you want to sort your head out?
>
> *I feel fearful, my heart is pounding, I can't catch my breath, I want desperately to get away and I can't move.*
> And just before you feel fearful and your heart is pounding?
>
> *Everything's fine, or at least, well no, it's not.*

Clare is accessing the AROUSAL and SENSATION stages of the feeling. As she learns to 'slow time down' around the rapid onset of the attacks, she begins to get a sense of a typical sequence to events. Gradually a pattern takes shape: the panic response appears in any situation where she finds herself feeling/thinking:

> *This is supposed to be ok, but isn't.*
> And when this is supposed to be ok, but isn't, that's like what?
>
> *Like a frantic hamster in a cage who's trying to escape but can't.*

"The logic of the emotional mind is associative," says Daniel Goleman. "It takes elements that symbolize a reality, or trigger a memory of it, to be the same as that reality. That is why similes, metaphors, and images speak directly to the emotional mind."

Clare is modelling her CONSTRUCTION of the feeling ("frantic hamster in a cage") via metaphor. She goes on to define the location of the metaphor's constituent symbols in space, to assign them a coding in time, and to discover their relationship to other symbols.

> And where is frantic hamster in a cage?
>
> *Just there* [points a meter in front of her].
> And is there anything else about just there?
>
> *I'm in the kitchen with the hamster and the garden's just outside.*
> And how old could 'I' be in the kitchen and the garden's just outside?
>
> *Um, four or five.*
> And when um four or five in the kitchen what happens next?
>
> [Pauses, then younger voice tone] *I want to get away into the garden even though they'll be really angry.*

Over the next few sessions, Clare explores the complete metaphor landscape of her anxiety. Suddenly she shifts into cognitive APPRAISAL as she is reminded of an incident in childhood when she had been abused by a carer who was a friend of the family.

> *I felt helpless. I was trapped. I wanted desperately to escape, but I was supposed to stay.*

She relates (re-appraises consciously) the child's helplessness to her panic responses as an adult. The feelings are the same: a pattern coded in the bind of wanting to escape but unable to.

Clare goes on to develop a symbolic resource – she calls it "gold liquid" – that she uses to convert her metaphor from a fixed wheel in a cage to a cycle of activity involving eddies of water and spirals of light. Not untypical of a self-generated resource: idiosyncratic, imaginative, and somehow it works, in a way that only its owner understands. The resource continues to develop and a few sessions later, Clare reports:

> *A week ago I had this weird epiphany thing. I could imagine these droplets of gold liquid going through my head. There used to be no movement, now I imagine this cycle thing going* [hand makes circular repeating gesture] *and I think, Ah, that's it! That's what it's like when my mind's working properly! I wrote and drew in my diary little gold droplets going round it like some sort of chemical. Now if I feel I'm about to panic and nothing's moving, I can think it and make it move.*

Transforming a wheel going nowhere into a cycle lubricated by droplets of gold is isomorphic with transforming the quality of her experience from helplessness and depression to control and self-assurance. It was no accident that Clare's original outcome, "To sort my head out," found its resolution in the symbolic mapping of events in her own mind. And gold liquid is a resource no therapist could have 'given' her. It was one that she had to construct, appraise, and evolve for herself.

The systems involved in emotional appraisal are directly involved in the control of emotional responses. In the final part of the paper, we look at their role in enhancing emotional intelligence.

Notes to Part IV

1 *'Low-level' and 'high-level' appraisal*: Paul E Griffiths, Basic Emotions, Complex Emotions and Machiavellian Emotions. Conference paper, Kings College London 2002

2 *Joyful or dreadful experience of a roller-coaster ride*. If a client's metaphor for life were 'a roller-coaster ride' or 'a constant uphill struggle' and their outcome were to transform it into 'a stroll in the park' or 'a level playing field,' the change in their metaphor landscape would be a significant measure of their re-appraisal of themselves.

AROUSAL   SENSATION   CONSTRUCTION   APPRAISAL   VOLITION
Part I   Part II   Part III   Part IV   Part V

Part V VOLITION

What first motivated my research into emotion and cognition was a profound dissatisfaction at my knowledge of how people do feelings. How do our brains construct these fundamental features of existence and how do they relate structurally to thoughts? I know now that emotions are essential for reason to operate with depth and intelligence. The process as a whole might more accurately be described as the construction of emocognition, in that the end result of these interlinked functions of the brain is their inseparable combination. We can have no emotion without the mind preconsciously appraising and labelling it (a cognitive process), and we can have no cognition without the body's prior involvement and influence (an emotional event). Indeed, the brain is embodied as much as the body is embrained.

In the fifth and final part of the paper, we consider what happens as a result of the four prior stages of emocognitive processing and discuss ways in which facilitators can utilize their awareness of volition in working with clients.

Volition derives from the Latin *volo*: I wish, I will, and is sometimes (loosely) defined as the act of freely willing or resolving. The more specific meaning I ascribe to it here is the impulse to act; the last moment before action itself. Part V is in three parts:

    ACTING ON IMPULSE   is free will ever voluntary?

    INVOLUNTARY IMPULSE   somatic markers – micro-emotions – metaphor

    VOLUNTARY IMPULSE   deconditioning – reprogramming – transforming therapies

and concludes with a note on emotional intelligence and the future.

ACTING ON IMPULSE
Most of our 'thinking' is 'wishful'. Alfred Korzybski

We call the wave of energy transmitted from neuron to neuron in the brain an 'electrical impulse.' In English, this relates neurolinguistically to two everyday meanings of impulse: a spontaneous inclination or desire ('a sudden impulse'); and a considered inspiration or drive ('the creative impulse'). Thus volition as the impulse to act may be involuntary or voluntary [Figure 1].

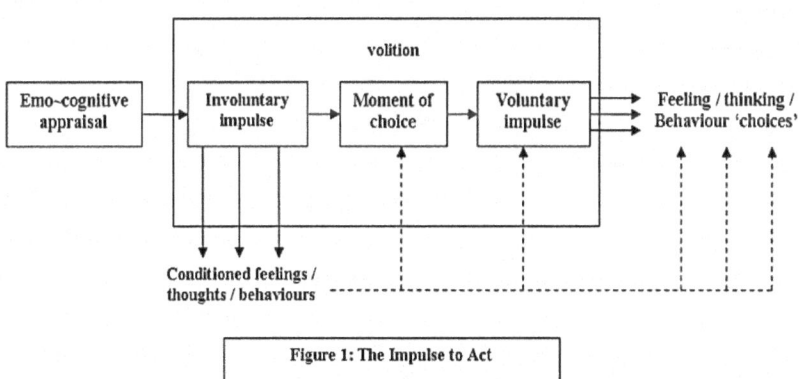

Figure 1: The Impulse to Act

The mind is an amalgam of sensation and appraisal, with volition the result. Volition has inclination, or intention, or both, and the outcome will be a conditioned response (reacting with apparently spontaneous fear to a perceived threat to survival, say); or a selected response (assessing the reality of the threat and controlling the reaction). Selected responses are more than emotion-influenced, they are emotion-directed. The dotted lines in Figure 1 (page 53) represent the out-of-awareness priming of voluntary process by prior involuntary events, rather like an underground root system conditions the growth and shape of the visible tree.

Because of this unconscious priming, it is possible to say with certainty that we can never make purely rational choices, because that would mean rationalizing every possible outcome of an action, an impossible feat. Only a feeling can limit the potentially infinite regress of reason. And feelings, as we saw in Part III, are the unpredictable offspring of the unconscious.

If the voluntary impulse of reason derives from every involuntary emotional process that precedes it, can 'free will' ever be freely arrived at? To put it another way, do we make up our minds, or do our minds make themselves up? None of our representations of self or our experiences of control and intention originate in consciousness, so a self that experiences freedom of choice must be party to an elaborate, if understandable, self-deception.

Neuroscientists Halligan and Oakley state that in many respects the conscious self operates only as a monitor or recorder (or, I might add, reviewer) of events that take place in the unconscious.[1] They stress that consciousness happens too late in our neurophysiology to affect the outcomes of the unconscious mental processes that produce *all* our thoughts and feelings, and further, that *everything* experienced in consciousness has already been formed in the unconscious.

Evidence of the resulting impulse to act is always available, even if no action ensues. Only sensory acuity, the perception of subtle somatic distinctions, is needed to detect it.

INVOLUNTARY IMPULSE
Somatic Markers   Micro-Emotions   Metaphor

Working with Somatic Markers
Basic emotions help manage actions in a rational way.   Antonio Damasio

Damasio's 'somatic marker hypothesis' calls upon the body's entire system of somatic and visceral feedback as a relevance testing or biasing device to reduce the need for sifting through endless possibilities. He describes it as a mechanism for arriving at the solution of a problem without reasoning toward it. A kind of gut/brain feeling, or rational-intuition.

How do we form our personal intuitions? I start from the presupposition that the organism seeks relative coherence in the face of changing external conditions (homeostasis) and is biased to avoid pain and seek pleasure. According to Damasio, where the choice of a certain option leads to a certain outcome and that outcome is followed by a pleasurable or painful body state, the brain acquires the hidden memory (or 'dispositional representation') of the experience: a non-inherited, subjective, involuntary association [Figure 2].

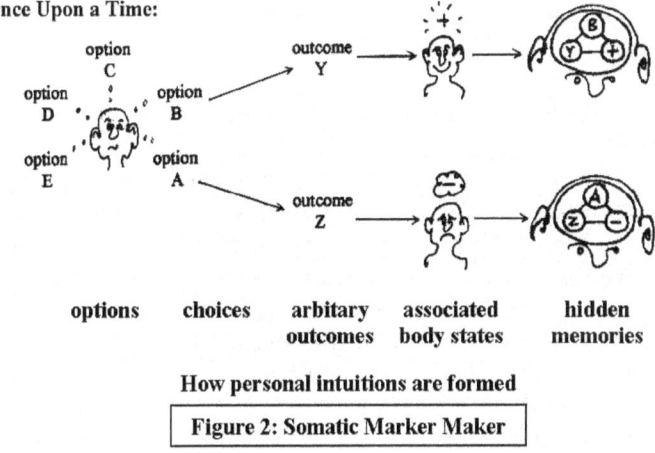

How personal intuitions are formed

Figure 2: Somatic Marker Maker

Re-exposure of the organism to the same option or thinking about the same outcome re-enacts the pleasurable or painful body state by re-activating the association, which serves as an involuntary ('intuitive') reminder of the outcome and heralds its likely – if by no means certain – reappearance [Figure 3].

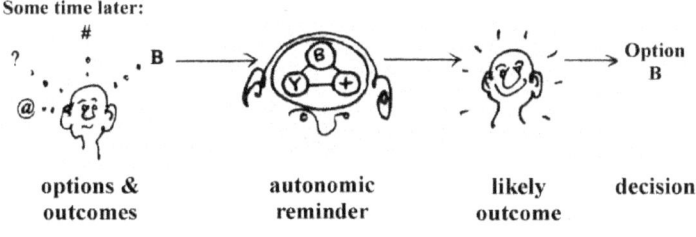

How personal intuitions are fulfilled

Figure 3: Somatic Decision Maker

Detecting somatic markers is not an infallible means of making 'correct', 'appropriate', or even 'adaptive' decisions, but a method of monitoring or assisting our subjective decision-making; a reminder that the responsibility we take for decisions is a deeply personal one; and an internal physiological check we can make to avoid the nightmare of not making decisions at all – provisos that apply equally to the facilitator as to the client. A facilitator's gut-brain feeling may prompt a decision about the next intervention, but only by keeping the intervention 'clean' can the facilitator be confident of not contaminating the client's response.

Working with Micro Emotions
It comes through my body.   Client

Emotional reactions show up in the musculature within a few thousandths of a second of the event that triggers them. They arrive in the form of unconsciously derived neuronal impulses to any muscle in the body as the body primes itself – just in case – to fight, flee, or freeze. These involuntary micro-emotions are a special sub-set of the nonverbal cues (gesture, posture, breathing, lines of sight, etc.) that can be utilized by a facilitator to encourage the emergence of new information for the client.

The exchange that follows is taken from a Clean Practise Group exercise facilitated by Caitlin Walker.[2] Note the lightning speed with which movements of this kind may manifest. The client's body may react to a word from the facilitator well before the question is completed or the client's mind has consciously appraised it.

The full syntax has been condensed. Nonverbal events [noted in brackets] happen concurrently with speech.

> Caitlin   And what would you like to have [client flinches almost imperceptibly] happen?
> Clive   *I'm not sure.*
>
> Caitlin   And what kind of [subtly mirrors flinch] I'm not sure could that be?
> Clive   *Hm. It comes through my body.*
>
> Caitlin   And hm it comes through your body [client: same micro-movement] like what?
> Clive   *Like a tornado.*
>
> Caitlin   [Subtly mirrors client movement] And what kind of tornado?
> Clive   [Blinks] *It's quite striking.*

Indeed. Tiny movements can be pointers to great events. They can easily be missed, or dismissed, because they look little different to the succession of turns and twitches we make every moment we are alive. A facilitator listening only for a client's verbal response or thinking ahead to the next question may easily miss a trick or two, because the only spacetime in which new information manifests and change shows through with any certainty – with no possibility of the client repressing, avoiding, or amending it – is this *preconscious micro-moment*. Reflecting it back to the client cleanly, without exaggerating the effect, is a delicate enterprise.

Clive's 'tornado' is, of course, a metaphor of feeling.

Working with Metaphor
I was in the grip of my emotions.   Client

There is a great deal more for a client to discover about feelings than is accessible from a retrospective thought or the twitch of a muscle. An intuitive description of the client's need for emotional control, say ("I need to tame," "curb," "battle with"), or a problem with emotional excess ("my feelings run riot," "they boil over"), will more often than not manifest in metaphor and suggest the presence of some kind of force or impulse in its construction.

How can this involuntary impulse be engaged? If we accept with Goleman that the logic of the emotional mind is associative – that it takes the representations of the reality it generates to be the same as that reality – then we can allow that the symbols and metaphors we use to describe our feelings are *just as they seem*. They may be taken quite literally and questioned as fact.

The use of client imagery in remedial work has a long history. The earliest Hindu healers believed that images were one of the ways that the gods sent messages to people. Hippocrates considered the imagination to be an actual corporeal organ of healing. Ernest Rossi in The Psychobiology of Mindbody Healing quotes Jung's belief that imagery formed during "active imagining" was about as close to the unconscious as one could get:

> When Jung's patients became overwhelmed with emotion, he would sometimes have them draw a picture of their feelings. Once the feelings were expressed in the form of imagery, the images could be encouraged to speak to one another. As soon as a dialogue could take place, the patient was well embarked on the process of reconciling different aspects of his [sic] dissociated psyche.

The exercise below utilizes self-generated imagery as a creative tool in emotional management.[3] It encourages Jung's "dialogue" to take place cleanly, without risk of contaminating the client's process with the therapist's assumptions, suggestions, and interpretations of meaning.

METAPHOR IN EMOTIONAL MANAGEMENT

1 ELICIT METAPHOR #1
Facilitator invites client to identify/select/generate a metaphor for an emotion which leads to them acting inappropriately:
"That is like what?"
Asks basic Clean questions of the metaphor and the symbols that make up the metaphor: "What kind of [X] is that [X]?" "Is there anything else about that [X]?" The intention is not to seek change, but for the client to get more information about the metaphor *as it is*. Facilitator invites client to map/draw Metaphor #1.

2 ELICIT METAPHOR #2
Facilitator invites client to generate a metaphor for how they would prefer to respond:
"That is like what?"
Asks basic Clean questions as step 1. Client maps Metaphor #2.

3 COMPARE
Facilitator invites client to consider Maps #1 & #2 by positioning them anywhere in the space and placing themself in relation to the maps. Asks client: "Within the context of the metaphor, how can Metaphor #1 BECOME Metaphor #2?"
Facilitates with basic Clean questions.

4 APPRAISE
Facilitator: "What is the FIRST thing that needs to happen for Metaphor #1 to become Metaphor #2?" Then: "What is the LAST thing that needs to happen?"
[If appropriate] Invites client to draw new Metaphor Map that symbolizes the whole process of #1 becoming #2 or to draw key 'In-betweens' like the intermediate frames of an animated film.

5 FUTURE PACE
Facilitator: "How will the information in the metaphor guide your behaviour next time you are in a similar situation?" "You can start getting used to being like Metaphor #2 by embodying its characteristics NOW." Asks: "What is your posture?" "What do you feel?" "Where is your focus of attention?" "What do you say and how?"

The use of Clean questioning in steps 1 – 4 allows the facilitator to honour not only the client's unconscious impulse, but also their experience of conscious, voluntary volition.

VOLUNTARY IMPULSE
Deconditioning   Reprogramming   Transforming

Reason, ruling alone, is a force confining; and passion, unattended, is a flame that burns to its own destruction.   Khalil Gibran

How may we voluntarily enhance our emotional intelligence as a result of understanding how we construct it involuntarily? Firstly, we need to accept that we are going to have painful or difficult feelings, whether we like it or not; they come with being alive. Secondly, we need to believe that our brains are not hard-wired immutably and may be changed. Thirdly, we need to rely less on the cognitive reporting of feelings, because a client's retrospective access to their cause or construction will be at best flimsy, and in any case, as we saw in Parts III and IV, the mind has no way of distinguishing reliably between the production of 'feeling' and 'thought' in the brain.

There are several alternative ways of dealing with difficult feelings without having to think about them. *Doing nothing* (going through life on an emotional wing and a prayer) is a common enough option, and pretty much guarantees distress at some time of life. *Suppression* (sitting on or denying feelings) is generally accepted as being bad for the health. *Body therapies* (yoga, shiatsu, acupuncture, etc.) and *'energy' therapies* (crystal twirling, dowsing, reiki), have an integrative intention, but leave most of the mind work to the caprice of the client. *Spiritual therapies* (shamanism, mysticism, animism) take little account of the body and are generally fuzzy in their application.

Deconditioning, reprogramming, and transforming therapies utilize the systemic capacities of the bodymind.

Deconditioning Therapies
Deconditioning (or 'extinction') therapies are mainly employed for manifestations of the fear response – anxiety, phobia, compulsive disorder – and in essence consist of the gradual presentation of the learned trigger or conditioned stimulus without the worst-case scenario reaction. The client gradually gets the idea that things aren't so bad after all. The techniques can be tricky to set up and

may be stressful in their early stages, but in many cases, with persistence, seem to work. However, the unconscious origins of the pattern that prompted the problem in the first place remain unexplored and it seems likely that its neuronal connections stay in place. This would explain why phobic-like behavioural and emotional reactions often erupt spontaneously long after they have been 'extinguished'.

Reprogramming Therapies
Recent research using brain imaging techniques confirms what NLP and hypnotic trance practitioners have known intuitively for years: that effective reprogramming changes the brain as much as drugs can. New neuronal firings create new programmes, new programmes prompt the neurons to fire differently – a systemic effect based on the simple principle of the bodymind loop [Figure 4]:

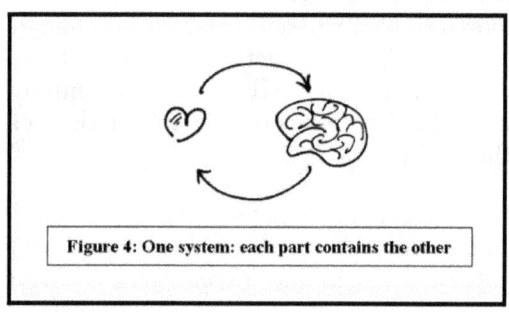

Figure 4: One system: each part contains the other

In his book Mind Sculpture, Ian Robertson offers a simple test of bodymind interdependency: "By an act of will or whimsy we can decide to change the state of our brains this moment by choosing to summon some sweet memory into consciousness." Recall of this kind is a voluntary volitional act. In NLP, it is called 'meta-stating' – superimposing or layering a resource state over the problem state in the expectation that the problem state will take on new qualities or at least waste away. Researcher Bob Bodenhamer invites us to try it out for ourselves in the moment:

> If you experience fear, what happens if you become fearful of your fear? You will become more fearful, maybe even paranoid. The fear of the original fear multiplies the first state. But what if you accepted your fear, what happens? The fear changes, doesn't it? And what happens if you apply faith, courage, compassion, understanding, etc. to your fear? [4]

We can all conjure up the semblance of a feeling within the brain and it will have much the same effect as a spontaneous body state.

Athletes improve their performances with mind 'rehearsal'. Intuitive actors feel their way into a character's thoughts. Intellectual actors think their way into a character's feelings. Brain scans show that 'thinking' a bodymind state is neurologically no different to having the state spontaneously.

Transforming Therapies

Change has a transforming effect when involuntary and voluntary knowing combine; when the organism functions, as Korzybski put it, "as-a-whole". It is at this moment that vital information imprisoned in the problem pattern is released and the bodymind is freed of its self-imposed shackles.

CASE HISTORY: BEN

This is an extract from a Clean Language and Therapeutic Metaphor process with a client in his thirties who came to therapy with what he described as an "overwhelming spider phobia." Ben's case, unique though it is, illustrates how any emocognitive construct can be accessed via Clean questioning at any of the five phases of its construction:

1 Arousal: Ben's reporting of sensory input into his system.

2 Sensation: his physiological responses to this arousal.

3 Construction: the unconscious associations to these sensations that he makes from past events, present goals, etc.

4 Appraisal: his internal assessment and labelling of these constructions.

5 Volition: his impulse to act on this appraisal.

Clients don't always communicate their emotional constructs in this convenient order, unfortunately. And Ben's awareness and communication of events will always lag behind the events themselves. Yet if you were to map the five-phase model across to the exchange with Ben, you would see that every statement or move he makes is a report of these five events happening over and over again. Every one of his feelings has to go through the three initial phases of arousal, sensation, and construction. Every one of his metaphors is a compact account of the third and fourth phases, construction and appraisal. Every tiny physiological shift is a signal of the fifth, volition. And it all happens in the moment.[5]

The Clean Language syntax of the facilitator has been condensed.

Ben	*It's so overwhelming, I can't be alone in the house with one. I read somewhere that people on average eat eight spiders in a lifetime, and that wherever you are you're never more than three feet away from one.* [Eyes widen] *If I see one in the house I'm terrified.*
Facilitator	And with all that what would you like to have happen?
Ben	*To be able to relax.*
Facilitator	And when you are able to relax, then what happens?
Ben	[Shoulders drop slightly] *A sense of peace and balance.*
Facilitator	And when a sense of peace and balance, then what happens?
Ben	*Feeling honoured and cared for.*
Facilitator	What kind of honoured and cared for?
Ben	[Slight frown] *Loved for who you are and as you are.*

At the next session, Ben brings a representation of some part of his construct in the form of a dream:

Ben	*It was about a window covered in webs, and I was really small compared to the window.*
Facilitator	And how old could 'I' be that was really small compared to the window?
Ben	[Younger voice tone] *Six or seven. The webs were very dirty.*
Facilitator	What kind of dirty?
Ben	*Layers. Years of webs. But there was no over-riding panic when the hoover didn't suck them up.* [Pause] *I could be quite fond of spiders. An odd thing to say, that. It would be nice not having to kill them.* [Shivers] *But if I see one at home ...*
Facilitator	And what happens just before you see one at home?
Ben	*I'm feeling jumpy, scared.*
Facilitator	Like what?
Ben	*Like being lost in the forest. A big old dark forest. Like Hansel and Gretel left by their parents, who were upright moral citizens.*
Facilitator	And what happens just before upright moral citizen parents left Hansel and Gretel?
Ben	[Pause] *They lost all their money, they couldn't afford their children, but Hansel and Gretel kept finding their way back again ...* [recalls] *... our house being possessed, moving into*

a caravan, being sent to boarding school paid for by an aunt. My mother tells me that me and my sister changed at that time. I had bad school reports, they were waved in my face. I was no good at exams. I only remember one thing from my Latin: 'puer in silva', boy in the woods ...

He maps out a thick green forest with a house glimpsed through the trees in the distance.

Facilitator What are you drawn to?

Ben *The house. It's light, warm, everyone is there, it's a party. I'm not wanted. I'm scared and lonely.* [Slight move back] *I keep my distance, like a lone wolf.*

Facilitator What kind of lone wolf?

Ben *The sort who goes off for a long time and comes back.* [Long pause] *I took the boy's hand, and smiled, and reassured him.*

In his third session:

Ben *I kind of thought yesterday I don't really have a problem with spiders and I don't know what the fuss was about. I've been thinking about whether the fear allows me to feel vulnerable and let other people sort out them out. Home should be a place of happiness and sociability but my home wasn't. It was there I was fearful of spiders.*

Facilitator And what would you like to have happen now?

Ben *To go into the garden and get a spider and bring it into the house.*

We go into the garden. He allows a spider to run over his hand. He watches it.

I have never ever done that before!

Ben coaxes the spider into a jar and we return to the consulting room. He keeps spider and jar close for the remainder of the session.

Two weeks later, in what turns out to be his final session:

> Ben   *I've thought a lot about the phobia being some sort of displacement for needing other people. I depended on my parents and I lost that when I was sent to boarding school. Now I'm linking spiders to a need in me to be less alone, less alien. I acknowledge spiders rather than avoid them. I'm getting to know them more. I've stopped thinking of spiders as alien.*

And two years after this work, he reports:

> *I've been in contact with many small spiders in the last two years and I'm little bothered by them. Instead of killing them or having someone dispose of them, I generally leave them alone, though sometimes I speak to them. A couple of times I have needed to pick up a big house spider in a glass and put it outside. Not a pleasant task, but possible.*

In his own way, Ben has brought feeling and thought, involuntary and voluntary impulse, pre-conscious and conscious knowing together to create a different volition. He has transformed "overwhelming fear" into "little bothered" without a single suggestion from the facilitator and has generated a range of behavioural, emotional, and cognitive choices for himself.

Concluding

You are not thinking, you are merely being logical.
Niels Bohr to Albert Einstein

Emotional intelligence is simply learning to use emotion intelligently and this happens when amygdala and cortex communicate well as one circuit. At our present stage of evolution, there happen to be many more neuronal connections from the brain's emotional centre (the amygdala) to its rational centre (the cortex) than there are the other way round. But we are not fixed entities. Neurobiologist Susan Greenfield suggests that as emotional intelligence evolves and the pre-frontal cortex becomes more active, neuronal connectivity from the cortex to the amygdala will increase and even up the present imbalance.

At the same time, the continuing survival value of the emotions as they cope with anything the world might throw at us will keep us from retreating into over-introspection: more grounded in the here and now, with greater self-awareness, healthier self-control, increased empathy with others, improved social skills, and enhanced personal influence.

It may be time to update the sentiment of the Greek poet who wrote, "Let my heart be wise, it is the gods' best gift." This is a gift that facilitators of all kinds can help people give themselves. Not just in the cause of individual fulfilment, but to help further the mutual trust, shared values, and common purpose that are the requisites for a progressive society.

© 2012 Philip Harland

Notes to Part V

1 *Conscious self as monitor or recorder of unconscious events*: Peter Halligan and David Oakley, 'What do you mean when you talk about "yourself?' New Scientist, 18 Nov 2000.

2 *Micro-emotions exercise*: the 'client' was Clive Bach.

3 *Metaphor in Emotional Management*: exercise created originally by Penny Tompkins and James Lawley, adapted with permission.

4 *'Meta-states' of feeling*: quotation from Bob Bodenhamer's review of Peter Young's Understanding NLP, Rapport 54 Winter 2001.

5 *Happening in the moment*: more on the momentary appearance and utilization of client information in Drama Behind The Scenes, Chapter 8 of Trust Me, I'm The Patient.

Acknowledgments
James Lawley, Penny Tompkins, Carol Thompson for their creativity and attention to detail.

Earlier versions of this paper appeared in Rapport, the journal of the UK Association for NLP; in Suppose, the journal of the Canadian Association of NLP; and at www.cleanlanguage.co.uk

References and Further Reading
Peter Afford, *The Neuroscience of Therapy,* The Psychotherapist Spring 2002
Leslie Cameron-Bandler and Michael Lebeau, *The Emotional Hostage,* Real People Press 1986
Antonio R Damasio, *Descartes' Error: Emotion, Reason and the Human Brain,* Putnam's 1994;
    The Feeling of What Happens: Body, Emotion & the Making of Consciousness, Heineman 1999
Daniel Goleman, *Emotional Intelligence,* Bloomsbury 1996
Susan Greenfield, *The Private Life of the Brain,* Penguin 2001
David Grove and Basil Panzer, *Resolving Traumatic Memories: Metaphors and Symbols in Psychotherapy,* Irvington 1989
L. Michael Hall, *Meta-States,* E.T. Publications 1995-2000
Philip Harland, *Trust Me, I'm The Patient,* Wayfinder Press 2012; *The Power of Six,* Wayfinder Press 2009
Bryony Lavery, *Frozen,* National Theatre London 2002
James Lawley and Penny Tompkins, *Metaphors in Mind: Transformation through Symbolic Modelling,* The Developing Company Press 2000
Joseph LeDoux, *The Emotional Brain,* Weidenfeld & Nicolson 1998
Stephen Porges, *The Polyvagal Theory: Neurophysiological Foundations of Emotions, Attachment, Communication, and Self-Regulation,* Norton 2011
Ian Robertson, *Mind Sculpture: Unleashing Your Brain's Potential,* Bantam 1999
And the following papers presented at *Emotion, Evolution, and Rationality,* an interdisciplinary conference hosted by the Philosophy Department, Kings College London 2002:
    Antonio Damasio, *A Neurobiology for Emotion and Feeling*
    Ray Dolan, *William James and Emotion Revisited*
    Dylan Evans, *The Search Hypothesis of Emotions*
    Paul Griffiths, *Basic Emotions, Complex Emotions and Machiavellian Emotions*
    Jim Hopkins and Christopher Badcock, *Emotion versus Reason as a Genetic Conflict*
    Andrew Lawrence, *Emotions and Evolution: Insights from Neuropsychology*
    Chandra Sripada and Stephen Stich, *Evolution, Culture and Irrationality of the Emotions*

Philip Harland is a psychotherapist specializing in Clean Language, Therapeutic Metaphor, and Emergent Knowledge. He is the author of *Trust Me, I'm The Patient: Clean Language, Metaphor, and The New Psychology of Change,* and *The Power of Six: A Six-Part Guide to Self Knowledge.* Contact via info@wayfinderpress.co.uk

www.ingramcontent.com/pod-product-compliance
Lightning Source LLC
Chambersburg PA
CBHW072015060426
42446CB00043B/2559